SHE RAN
A Marathoner's Journal

She Ran: A Marathoner's Journal by Shannon Banks Sapp

Published by Kaleidoblaze, an Imprint of Wingdon Books
http://www.wingdonbooks.com

For permissions contact:
permissions@wingdonbooks.com

ISBN: 979-8-9899570-9-5 (paperback)

Printed in The United States of America

First Edition

Warm-Up

She Ran: A Marathoner's Devotions documents the preparation for Shannon Banks Sapp's fifteenth 26.2: Albuquerque's Duke City Marathon. For every day of the process, whether it's a running day, cross-training day, or rest day, she included what she believes to be a relevant passage from Scripture, along with her own observations. It is a training log and testimony; it is a roadmap and reflection. If you haven't yet read it, pick it up and follow along every day as you fill out this journal.

This journal is meant to accompany *She Ran* and provide you with an opportunity to document your own journey: in running, in faith and in life.

There are pages every day for you to keep track of what is happening in your life and faith, what you ran that day, how you felt, overall conditions, and more.

Through keeping track of how you are feeling and what you are doing, you will be able to see your growth and progress, learn what works and what doesn't, and progress toward your goals.

Whether you're training for a marathon right now or you're simply begining on this running and faith journey, welcome.

Now, let's lace up.

Day 1

My Spiritual Log

_____

_____

_____

_____

_____

_____

_____

_____

_____

_____

_____

_____

_____

_____

She Ran

My Daily Running Log

Distance

Terrain

Pace

Weather

Overall Feeling

Observations

A Marathoner's Journal

Day 2

My Spiritual Log

My Daily Running Log

Distance

Terrain

Pace

Weather

Overall Feeling

Observations

A Marathoner's Journal

Day 3

My Spiritual Log

My Daily Running Log

Distance

Terrain

Pace

Weather

Overall Feeling

Observations

Day 4

My Spiritual Log

My Daily Running Log

Distance

Terrain

Pace

Weather

Overall Feeling

Observations

Day 5

My Spiritual Log

My Daily Running Log

Distance

_____

_____

Terrain

_____

_____

Pace

_____

_____

Weather

_____

_____

Overall Feeling

_____

_____

_____

Observations

_____

_____

_____

_____

Day 6

My Spiritual Log

My Daily Running Log

Distance

Terrain

Pace

Weather

Overall Feeling

Observations

A Marathoner's Journal

Day 7

My Spiritual Log

My Daily Running Log

Distance

Terrain

Pace

Weather

Overall Feeling

Observations

A Marathoner's Journal

Day 8

My Spiritual Log

My Daily Running Log

Distance

Terrain

Pace

Weather

Overall Feeling

Observations

A Marathoner's Journal

Day 9

My Spiritual Log

My Daily Running Log

Distance

Terrain

Pace

Weather

Overall Feeling

Observations

Day 10

My Spiritual Log

My Daily Running Log

Distance

Terrain

Pace

Weather

Overall Feeling

Observations

Day 11

My Spiritual Log

My Daily Running Log

Distance

Terrain

Pace

Weather

Overall Feeling

Observations

A Marathoner's Journal

Day 12

My Spiritual Log

_____

_____

_____

_____

_____

_____

_____

_____

_____

_____

_____

_____

_____

_____

My Daily Running Log

Distance

Terrain

Pace

Weather

Overall Feeling

Observations

A Marathoner's Journal

Day 13

My Spiritual Log

My Daily Running Log

Distance

Terrain

Pace

Weather

Overall Feeling

Observations

A Marathoner's Journal

Day 14

My Spiritual Log

My Daily Running Log

Distance

Terrain

Pace

Weather

Overall Feeling

Observations

A Marathoner's Journal

Day 15

My Spiritual Log

My Daily Running Log

Distance

Terrain

Pace

Weather

Overall Feeling

Observations

Day 16

My Spiritual Log

My Daily Running Log

Distance

Terrain

Pace

Weather

Overall Feeling

Observations

A Marathoner's Journal

Day 17

My Spiritual Log

My Daily Running Log

Distance

Terrain

Pace

Weather

Overall Feeling

Observations

A Marathoner's Journal

Day 18

My Spiritual Log

My Daily Running Log

Distance

Terrain

Pace

Weather

Overall Feeling

Observations

A Marathoner's Journal

Day 19

My Spiritual Log

My Daily Running Log

Distance

Terrain

Pace

Weather

Overall Feeling

Observations

Day 20

My Spiritual Log

My Daily Running Log

Distance

Terrain

Pace

Weather

Overall Feeling

Observations

A Marathoner's Journal

Day 21

My Spiritual Log

My Daily Running Log

Distance

Terrain

Pace

Weather

Overall Feeling

Observations

A Marathoner's Journal

Day 22

My Spiritual Log

My Daily Running Log

Distance

_____

_____

Terrain

_____

_____

Pace

_____

_____

Weather

_____

_____

Overall Feeling

_____

_____

_____

Observations

_____

_____

_____

_____

A Marathoner's Journal

Day 23

My Spiritual Log

My Daily Running Log

Distance

Terrain

Pace

Weather

Overall Feeling

Observations

A Marathoner's Journal

Day 24

My Spiritual Log

My Daily Running Log

Distance

Terrain

Pace

Weather

Overall Feeling

Observations

Day 25

My Spiritual Log

My Daily Running Log

Distance

Terrain

Pace

Weather

Overall Feeling

Observations

A Marathoner's Journal

Day 26

My Spiritual Log

My Daily Running Log

Distance

_____

_____

Terrain

_____

_____

Pace

_____

_____

Weather

_____

_____

Overall Feeling

_____

_____

_____

Observations

_____

_____

_____

_____

A Marathoner's Journal

Day 27

My Spiritual Log

My Daily Running Log

Distance

Terrain

Pace

Weather

Overall Feeling

Observations

Day 28

My Spiritual Log

My Daily Running Log

Distance

Terrain

Pace

Weather

Overall Feeling

Observations

A Marathoner's Journal

Day 29

My Spiritual Log

My Daily Running Log

Distance

Terrain

Pace

Weather

Overall Feeling

Observations

A Marathoner's Journal

Day 30

My Spiritual Log

My Daily Running Log

Distance

Terrain

Pace

Weather

Overall Feeling

Observations

A Marathoner's Journal

Day 31

My Spiritual Log

My Daily Running Log

Distance

Terrain

Pace

Weather

Overall Feeling

Observations

A Marathoner's Journal

Day 32

My Spiritual Log

She Ran

My Daily Running Log

Distance

Terrain

Pace

Weather

Overall Feeling

Observations

A Marathoner's Journal

Day 33

My Spiritual Log

My Daily Running Log

Distance

Terrain

Pace

Weather

Overall Feeling

Observations

A Marathoner's Journal

Day 34

My Spiritual Log

My Daily Running Log

Distance

Terrain

Pace

Weather

Overall Feeling

Observations

A Marathoner's Journal

Day 35

My Spiritual Log

My Daily Running Log

Distance

Terrain

Pace

Weather

Overall Feeling

Observations

Day 36

My Spiritual Log

My Daily Running Log

Distance

Terrain

Pace

Weather

Overall Feeling

Observations

A Marathoner's Journal

Day 37

My Spiritual Log

My Daily Running Log

Distance

Terrain

Pace

Weather

Overall Feeling

Observations

Day 38

My Spiritual Log

My Daily Running Log

Distance

_____

_____

Terrain

_____

_____

Pace

_____

_____

Weather

_____

_____

Overall Feeling

_____

_____

_____

Observations

_____

_____

_____

_____

A Marathoner's Journal

Day 39

My Spiritual Log

My Daily Running Log

Distance

_____

_____

Terrain

_____

_____

Pace

_____

_____

Weather

_____

_____

Overall Feeling

_____

_____

_____

Observations

_____

_____

_____

_____

A Marathoner's Journal

Day 40

My Spiritual Log

My Daily Running Log

Distance

Terrain

Pace

Weather

Overall Feeling

Observations

A Marathoner's Journal

Day 41

My Spiritual Log

My Daily Running Log

Distance

Terrain

Pace

Weather

Overall Feeling

Observations

A Marathoner's Journal

Day 42

My Spiritual Log

My Daily Running Log

Distance

_____

_____

Terrain

_____

_____

Pace

_____

_____

Weather

_____

_____

Overall Feeling

_____

_____

_____

Observations

_____

_____

_____

_____

A Marathoner's Journal

Day 43

My Spiritual Log

My Daily Running Log

Distance

Terrain

Pace

Weather

Overall Feeling

Observations

Day 44

My Spiritual Log

She Ran

My Daily Running Log

Distance

Terrain

Pace

Weather

Overall Feeling

Observations

Day 45

My Spiritual Log

My Daily Running Log

Distance

_____

_____

Terrain

_____

_____

Pace

_____

_____

Weather

_____

_____

Overall Feeling

_____

_____

_____

Observations

_____

_____

_____

A Marathoner's Journal

Day 46

My Spiritual Log

My Daily Running Log

Distance

Terrain

Pace

Weather

Overall Feeling

Observations

A Marathoner's Journal

Day 47

My Spiritual Log

My Daily Running Log

Distance

Terrain

Pace

Weather

Overall Feeling

Observations

A Marathoner's Journal

Day 48

My Spiritual Log

She Ran

My Daily Running Log

Distance

Terrain

Pace

Weather

Overall Feeling

Observations

A Marathoner's Journal

Day 49

My Spiritual Log

My Daily Running Log

Distance

Terrain

Pace

Weather

Overall Feeling

Observations

A Marathoner's Journal

Day 50

My Spiritual Log

My Daily Running Log

Distance

Terrain

Pace

Weather

Overall Feeling

Observations

A Marathoner's Journal

Day 51

My Spiritual Log

My Daily Running Log

Distance

Terrain

Pace

Weather

Overall Feeling

Observations

A Marathoner's Journal

Day 52

My Spiritual Log

My Daily Running Log

Distance

Terrain

Pace

Weather

Overall Feeling

Observations

A Marathoner's Journal

Day 53

My Spiritual Log

My Daily Running Log

Distance

Terrain

Pace

Weather

Overall Feeling

Observations

A Marathoner's Journal

Day 54

My Spiritual Log

My Daily Running Log

Distance

Terrain

Pace

Weather

Overall Feeling

Observations

A Marathoner's Journal

Day 55

My Spiritual Log

My Daily Running Log

Distance

Terrain

Pace

Weather

Overall Feeling

Observations

Day 56

My Spiritual Log

My Daily Running Log

Distance

_____

_____

Pace

_____

_____

Terrain

_____

_____

Weather

_____

_____

Overall Feeling

_____

_____

_____

Observations

_____

_____

_____

_____

A Marathoner's Journal

Day 57

My Spiritual Log

My Daily Running Log

Distance

Terrain

Pace

Weather

Overall Feeling

Observations

A Marathoner's Journal

Day 58

My Spiritual Log

My Daily Running Log

Distance

Terrain

Pace

Weather

Overall Feeling

Observations

A Marathoner's Journal

Day 59

My Spiritual Log

My Daily Running Log

Distance

Terrain

Pace

Weather

Overall Feeling

Observations

A Marathoner's Journal

Day 60

My Spiritual Log

My Daily Running Log

Distance

Terrain

Pace

Weather

Overall Feeling

Observations

Day 61

My Spiritual Log

My Daily Running Log

Distance

_____

_____

Pace

_____

_____

Terrain

_____

_____

Weather

_____

Overall Feeling

_____

_____

_____

Observations

_____

_____

_____

_____

A Marathoner's Journal

Day 62

My Spiritual Log

My Daily Running Log

Distance

Terrain

Pace

Weather

Overall Feeling

Observations

A Marathoner's Journal

Day 63

My Spiritual Log

My Daily Running Log

Distance

Terrain

Pace

Weather

Overall Feeling

Observations

A Marathoner's Journal

Day 64

My Spiritual Log

My Daily Running Log

Distance

Terrain

Pace

Weather

Overall Feeling

Observations

A Marathoner's Journal

Day 65

My Spiritual Log

My Daily Running Log

Distance

Terrain

Pace

Weather

Overall Feeling

Observations

A Marathoner's Journal

Day 66

My Spiritual Log

My Daily Running Log

Distance

Terrain

Pace

Weather

Overall Feeling

Observations

A Marathoner's Journal

Day 67

My Spiritual Log

My Daily Running Log

Distance

Terrain

Pace

Weather

Overall Feeling

Observations

Day 68

My Spiritual Log

My Daily Running Log

Distance

_____

_____

Terrain

_____

_____

Pace

_____

_____

Weather

_____

_____

Overall Feeling

_____

_____

_____

_____

Observations

_____

_____

_____

_____

_____

A Marathoner's Journal

Day 69

My Spiritual Log

_____

_____

_____

_____

_____

_____

_____

_____

_____

_____

_____

_____

_____

_____

My Daily Running Log

Distance

Terrain

Pace

Weather

Overall Feeling

Observations

A Marathoner's Journal

Day 70

My Spiritual Log

My Daily Running Log

Distance

Terrain

Pace

Weather

Overall Feeling

Observations

A Marathoner's Journal

Day 71

My Spiritual Log

My Daily Running Log

Distance

Terrain

Pace

Weather

Overall Feeling

Observations

A Marathoner's Journal

Day 72

My Spiritual Log

My Daily Running Log

Distance

Terrain

Pace

Weather

Overall Feeling

Observations

A Marathoner's Journal

Day 73

My Spiritual Log

My Daily Running Log

Distance

Terrain

Pace

Weather

Overall Feeling

Observations

A Marathoner's Journal

Day 74

My Spiritual Log

My Daily Running Log

Distance

Terrain

Pace

Weather

Overall Feeling

Observations

A Marathoner's Journal

Day 75

My Spiritual Log

My Daily Running Log

Distance

Terrain

Pace

Weather

Overall Feeling

Observations

A Marathoner's Journal

Day 76

My Spiritual Log

She Ran

My Daily Running Log

Distance

Terrain

Pace

Weather

Overall Feeling

Observations

Day 77

My Spiritual Log

My Daily Running Log

Distance

Terrain

Pace

Weather

Overall Feeling

Observations

A Marathoner's Journal

Day 78

My Spiritual Log

My Daily Running Log

Distance

Terrain

Pace

Weather

Overall Feeling

Observations

Day 79

My Spiritual Log

My Daily Running Log

Distance

Terrain

Pace

Weather

Overall Feeling

Observations

A Marathoner's Journal

Day 80

My Spiritual Log

My Daily Running Log

Distance

Terrain

Pace

Weather

Overall Feeling

Observations

A Marathoner's Journal

Day 81

My Spiritual Log

My Daily Running Log

Distance

Terrain

Pace

Weather

Overall Feeling

Observations

A Marathoner's Journal

Day 82

My Spiritual Log

My Daily Running Log

Distance

Terrain

Pace

Weather

Overall Feeling

Observations

A Marathoner's Journal

Day 83

My Spiritual Log

She Ran

My Daily Running Log

Distance

Terrain

Pace

Weather

Overall Feeling

Observations

A Marathoner's Journal

Day 84

My Spiritual Log

My Daily Running Log

Distance

Terrain

Pace

Weather

Overall Feeling

Observations

A Marathoner's Journal

Day 85

My Spiritual Log

My Daily Running Log

Distance

Terrain

Pace

Weather

Overall Feeling

Observations

Day 86

My Spiritual Log

My Daily Running Log

Distance

Terrain

Pace

Weather

Overall Feeling

Observations

A Marathoner's Journal

Day 87

My Spiritual Log

She Ran

My Daily Running Log

Distance

Terrain

Pace

Weather

Overall Feeling

Observations

Day 88

My Spiritual Log

My Daily Running Log

Distance

Terrain

Pace

Weather

Overall Feeling

Observations

A Marathoner's Journal

Day 89

My Spiritual Log

My Daily Running Log

Distance

Terrain

Pace

Weather

Overall Feeling

Observations

A Marathoner's Journal

Day 90

My Spiritual Log

My Daily Running Log

Distance

Terrain

Pace

Weather

Overall Feeling

Observations

A Marathoner's Journal

Day 91

My Spiritual Log

My Daily Running Log

Distance

Terrain

Pace

Weather

Overall Feeling

Observations

A Marathoner's Journal

Day 92

My Spiritual Log

My Daily Running Log

Distance

_____

_____

Pace

_____

_____

Terrain

_____

_____

Weather

_____

_____

Overall Feeling

_____

_____

_____

Observations

_____

_____

_____

_____

_____

A Marathoner's Journal

Day 93

My Spiritual Log

My Daily Running Log

Distance

Terrain

Pace

Weather

Overall Feeling

Observations

A Marathoner's Journal

Day 94

My Spiritual Log

My Daily Running Log

Distance

Terrain

Pace

Weather

Overall Feeling

Observations

Day 95

My Spiritual Log

My Daily Running Log

Distance

_____

_____

Terrain

_____

_____

Pace

_____

_____

Weather

_____

_____

Overall Feeling

_____

_____

_____

Observations

_____

_____

_____

_____

A Marathoner's Journal

Day 96

My Spiritual Log

My Daily Running Log

Distance

_____

_____

Pace

_____

_____

Terrain

_____

_____

Weather

_____

_____

Overall Feeling

_____

_____

_____

Observations

_____

_____

_____

_____

A Marathoner's Journal

Day 97

My Spiritual Log

My Daily Running Log

Distance

Terrain

Pace

Weather

Overall Feeling

Observations

A Marathoner's Journal

Day 98

My Spiritual Log

My Daily Running Log

Distance

Terrain

Pace

Weather

Overall Feeling

Observations

A Marathoner's Journal

Day 99

My Spiritual Log

My Daily Running Log

Distance

Terrain

Pace

Weather

Overall Feeling

Observations

A Marathoner's Journal

Day 100

My Spiritual Log

My Daily Running Log

Distance

Terrain

Pace

Weather

Overall Feeling

Observations

A Marathoner's Journal

Day 101

My Spiritual Log

She Ran

My Daily Running Log

Distance

Terrain

Pace

Weather

Overall Feeling

Observations

A Marathoner's Journal

Day 102

My Spiritual Log

My Daily Running Log

Distance

Terrain

Pace

Weather

Overall Feeling

Observations

A Marathoner's Journal

Day 103

My Spiritual Log

She Ran

My Daily Running Log

Distance

Terrain

Pace

Weather

Overall Feeling

Observations

A Marathoner's Journal

Day 104

My Spiritual Log

She Ran

My Daily Running Log

Distance

Terrain

Pace

Weather

Overall Feeling

Observations

Day 105

My Spiritual Log

My Daily Running Log

Distance

Terrain

Pace

Weather

Overall Feeling

Observations

Day 106

My Spiritual Log

My Daily Running Log

Distance

Terrain

Pace

Weather

Overall Feeling

Observations

A Marathoner's Journal

Day 107

My Spiritual Log

My Daily Running Log

Distance

Terrain

Pace

Weather

Overall Feeling

Observations

A Marathoner's Journal

Cool Down

After a major event like a marathon, one expects to feel different somehow. One expects their body, after all that, to have changed.

It's always a surprise to learn that it hasn't. Not really.

It's your mind that changes. It's your spirit. After a little recovery time, your body returns to how it was. Your heart of hearts? No. Never. Because, you *learned* something in that marathon. And maybe this something has actually been inside you all along; it just took running *this* particular marathon on *that* particular day to unearth it.

It's not about the time. It's not about awards or PRs or whether you smile for the cameras. It's not even about the t-shirt.

It's about continuing to realize the width and the depth of the spirit within you. The stamina. The peace. The strength. The compassion. The grit. The grace.

The *God*.

"Continuing to realize" because, you're not done. No one is. Opening yourself to God's love for you and His presence within you, and letting it shine out of you, is your life's work.

It's a marathon. The very best kind.

Let's lace up.

God bless you.

SHE RAN
A Marathoner's Journal

Kaleidoblaze, an Imprint of Wingdon Books, brings you some of the best non-fiction: Bible Study, Self Improvement, Biographical, etc... works.

While many stories are whimsical and fun works of fiction, some of the most transformative tales are those that are true. Kaleidoblaze brings you these true stories of personal and spiritual wisdom, insight and development.

To stay up to date on Kaleidoblaze and all of Wingdon Books' upcoming news and releases, sign-up for our email list at: www.wingdonbooks.com

Albuquerque, New Mexico

About The Author

Shannon lives in Albuquerque, New Mexico with her husband and two daughters. She has been a runner since 1995 and a writer off and on since childhood. She graduated from the College of William & Mary with a degree in English, and worked in editing until the birth of her first child.

Shannon continued to write and run through the early years of motherhood, and it was during this time that she began to feel compelled to explore her faith. She has found God and running inextricably linked. Writing about her personal journey in both running and faith is her humble offering to the Kingdom.

Nowadays she can almost always be found with a pair of running shoes and a Bible nearby. *She Ran* is her first book.

Follow Shannon's blog at http://www.runningsunflower.wordpress.com or find her on Instagram at https://www.instagram.com/running_sunflower.